CORE WRITING SKILLS

How to
Gather Information, Take Notes, and Sort Evidence

Sara Howell

New York

Published in 2014 by The Rosen Publishing Group, Inc.
29 East 21st Street, New York, NY 10010

First Edition

Editor: Amelie von Zumbusch
Book Design: Andrew Povolny
Photo Research: Katie Stryker

Photo Credits: Cover p. 4 Daniel Grill/Getty Images; p. 5 Wildnerdpix/Shutterstock.com; p. 6 Akiko Aoki/Flickr/Getty Images; p. 8 Brian Summers/First Light/Getty Images; p. 9 archana bhartia/Shutterstock.com; pp. 10–11, 22 Monkey Business Images/Shutterstock.com; p. 12 Photo Smile/Shutterstock.com; p. 13 Robert Ginn/Photolibrary/Getty Images; p. 14 JGI/Jamie Grill/Blend Images/Getty Images; p. 16 Jeff Gross/Getty Images Sport/Getty Images; p. 18 Vicky Kasala/Photodisc/Getty Images; p. 19 nmedia/Shutterstock.com; pp. 20–21 Dawn Shearer-Simonetti/Shutterstock.com.

Library of Congress Cataloging-in-Publication Data

Howell, Sara.
  How to gather information, take notes, and sort evidence / By Sara Howell. — First Edition.
    pages cm. — (Core writing skills)
  Includes index.
  ISBN 978-1-4777-2909-0 (library) — ISBN 978-1-4777-2998-4 (pbk.) —
  ISBN 978-1-4777-3068-3 (6-pack)
  1. Research—Methodology—Juvenile literature. 2. Library research—Juvenile literature. 3. Information literacy—Juvenile literature. 4. Information resources—Juvenile literature. 5. Note-taking—Juvenile literature. 6. Reference books—Juvenile literature. I. Title.
  ZA3080.H69 2014
  001.4'2—dc23
                                        2013023457

Manufactured in the United States of America

CPSIA Compliance Information: Batch #W14PK4: For Further Information contact Rosen Publishing, New York, New York at 1-800-237-9932

CONTENTS

Starting at the Beginning	4
Gathering the Information Around You	6
The Printed Word	8
Digital Sources	10
Facts and Fiction	12
Taking Notes	14
Sorting Evidence	16
In Your Own Words	18
Working Together	20
Sharing Your Finished Piece	22
Glossary	23
Index	24
Websites	24

STARTING AT THE BEGINNING

Imagine your teacher asked you to write a report on grizzly bears. How would you begin? First, you would find out everything you could about the **topic**. Then you would decide which information was important. Finally, you would sort the important information into groups and begin writing.

It is much easier to write a report when you have taken good notes and sorted your information clearly.

If you were writing about grizzly bears, you would want to find out where they live, what they eat, how they act around other grizzlies, and more.

Writing Tip

The writing skills you will learn in this book are useful for any type of writing in which you must find and present facts, such as opinion pieces.

As a student, you will often be asked to present information in explanatory texts. Some topics you write about may be familiar. Others will be completely new to you. Learning how to gather information, take notes, and sort evidence will help you plan and **organize** your texts before you even begin writing!

GATHERING THE INFORMATION AROUND YOU

Before you begin gathering information on your topic, you must first know where to look. In some cases, your best information might come from asking people questions and recording their answers. This is called an **interview**. You could interview your parents to write a piece about your grandmother's life.

If you want to interview somebody who lives far away, you can call that person on the phone.

Weather Chart

Date	Weather	Temperature
		79° F
June 4	Sunny	85° F
June 5	Sunny	82° F
June 6	Partly Cloudy	81° F
June 7	Rainy	83° F
June 8	Sunny	88° F
June 9	Partly Cloudy	

It can be helpful to make a chart like the one here when you are recording your observations about the world around you.

Writing Tip

When you are recording information, be sure that your instruments, such as thermometers and rain gauges, work well. Broken instruments will give you incorrect results!

In other cases, you can gather information by **observing** the world around you. If you were writing about the weather in your neighborhood, you could keep a journal of each day's clouds and rainfall. If you were writing about stars, you could use a telescope to observe their movements in the night sky.

THE PRINTED WORD

Books and other printed **sources**, such as newspapers, are great places to find information. Whatever your topic, there is probably a book about it! Find books written for your age and reading level. **Encyclopedias** cover a wide range of subjects, usually in alphabetical order. Newspaper articles are great sources for information about current events.

School libraries and public libraries are both great places to look for printed sources.

Sometimes sources may disagree on certain facts. An older book may say one thing, while a newer book will give you newer and more **accurate**, or correct, information. It is important that you always compare sources. Try to find at least two sources to back up any facts you use.

Writing Tip

Ask a librarian to help you find the right books, encyclopedias, and newspaper articles that you need to gather information.

If you are looking for information about recent events in your town, try looking in a local newspaper.

DIGITAL SOURCES

Books may take many months to be published and make their way to your local library. The Internet carries information to your computer in seconds. This can make the information very up-to-date. Finding information on the Internet is similar to searching in a library. You need to know where to look!

Begin by typing your topic into a **search engine**, such as Google. The search engine will give you a list of websites related to the topic. Some websites may ask you to register before you can see the site's information. Never put any personal information online without an adult's permission, though.

Writing Tip

Many encyclopedias also have an online edition. Go to the encyclopedia's website and type your topic into the search box.

Adding extra words to a web search can narrow your results. Typing "jaguar animal" will make sure you get websites about the wild cats, not the car company of the same name.

FACTS AND FICTION

The Internet is full of useful information. However, it is important to understand that not all the information on the Internet is true. When you are gathering information, look for websites run by **credible** sources. These can include museums, zoos, and the US government. For example, if you are looking for information about energy usage, try starting with the website run by the Department of Energy.

Do not assume that everything online is true. If you think a website does not seem credible, don't use it as a source.

This boy is visiting the Smithsonian Institution in Washington, DC. It includes 19 museums and galleries, as well as the National Zoo. Its websites are great sources of information.

Writing Tip

Be sure your information is current, or up-to-date. Credible sources usually keep their information current, while other sites may not.

The ending of a website's address is a useful clue to decide if it is credible. Government websites end with ".gov." Nonprofit groups use ".org" and college and university websites end with ".edu."

TAKING NOTES

As you read through books and websites or conduct interviews, it is important to write down useful facts that you see or hear. This is called taking notes. Your notes should be brief, or short, and include only the most important information.

Keeping your notes organized will make it easier to sort, or group, the information later. An **outline** uses letters, numbers, or bullet points to list ideas and facts. You can also use pens with different-colored ink to organize ideas. For example, facts about an animal's diet can be written in blue and facts about its appearance in red.

Concentrate on the most important facts when you are taking notes. Remember, you shouldn't write down every single piece of information the source contains.

Thomas Edison

A. Birth and Family
1. Born on February 11, 1847
2. Born in Milan, Ohio
3. Parents were Samuel Edison + Nancy Elliott Edison
4. Youngest of seven children

B. Education
1. Went to school for just a short time
2. Teachers thought he was not smart
3. Made lab at home for experiments

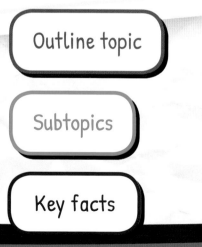

Outline topic

Subtopics

Key facts

Writing Tip

Do not worry about writing in complete sentences when taking notes or making an outline. Just write down key words and ideas.

SORTING EVIDENCE

Once you have gathered your information in brief notes, it is time to sort it into **categories**, or groups. One way to do this is to use index or note cards. Think of each index card as a separate paragraph in your report. What questions would you like the paragraphs to answer?

If you are writing about a sports team, you might sort information about the players on the team by the positions they play.

Where do bald eagles live?

- Only in North America
- By "lakes, reservoirs, rivers, marshes, and coasts"

http://www.allaboutbirds.org/guide/Bald_Eagle/id

Topic question

Facts

Source

If you are writing about insects, you might have questions such as "What do insects look like?" and "Where do insects live?" Write each question at the top of an index card. Then read through your notes and copy down the facts that answer the question.

Writing Tip

If you are writing about an event, try using your index cards to answer the questions who what, when, where, why, and how.

IN YOUR OWN WORDS

How would you feel if one of your classmates copied your report and handed it in as her own? Taking someone else's work and calling it your own is called **plagiarism**. Plagiarism can be cutting and pasting an entire article or copying just a few sentences. Though it may seem harmless, plagiarism is actually a form of stealing!

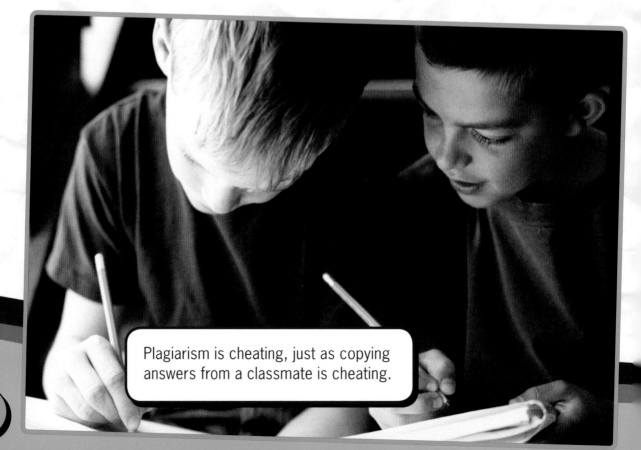

Plagiarism is cheating, just as copying answers from a classmate is cheating.

Make sure to include the websites you use in your bibliography as well. Bibliographies include more than just books!

Writing Tip

Some words or phrases, such as quotes, do need to be copied exactly. To do this, put the phrase inside quotation marks and tell readers who said it or wrote it.

To avoid plagiarism in your writing, always name your sources. If you learned from a book that emperor penguins live in Antarctica, list that book as a source at the end of your report. This list of your sources is called a **bibliography**.

WORKING TOGETHER

Sometimes teachers will assign a small group to work together on a research and writing project. Working with others is a fun way to learn from each other and share responsibilities.

As you begin your project, get together and talk about each group member's strengths. One person may be good at taking notes. Another may have strong keyboarding skills. You can use these strengths to divide the work and decide on everyone's role, or job. Make sure the work is shared equally and everyone understands what he or she needs to do. As you work together, listen to each other's ideas, problems, and questions.

Writing Tip

Many groups benefit from having a leader. This person may lead group talks and check on how everyone's work is coming along.

When working on a group project, you will likely spend some time working alone and some time working with others in your group.

SHARING YOUR FINISHED PIECE

The more you practice gathering information, taking notes, and sorting evidence, the better you will become. These skills will help you write a report that is organized and conveys ideas and information clearly.

When your report is finished, you can use technology, such as computers and the Internet, to share it with others. Try starting your own website about your topic. Other students may even use your website as a source for their own reports!

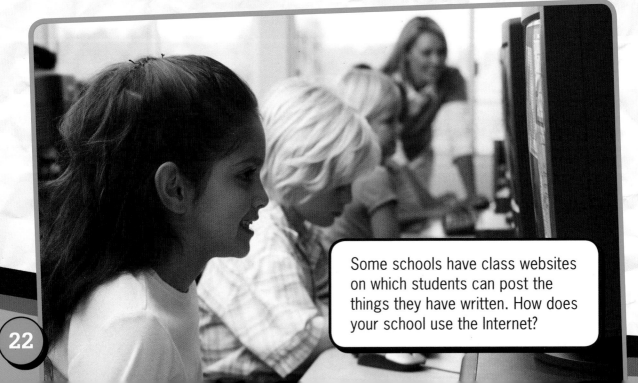

Some schools have class websites on which students can post the things they have written. How does your school use the Internet?

GLOSSARY

accurate (A-kyuh-rut) Exactly right.

bibliography (bih-blee-O-gruh-fee) A list of the sources used or quoted in a piece of writing.

categories (KA-teh-gor-eez) Groups of things that are alike.

credible (KREH-duh-bel) Believable and trustworthy.

encyclopedias (in-sy-kluh-PEE-dee-uhz) Books that have information about a wide range of subjects, usually in alphabetical order.

interview (IN-ter-vyoo) When someone questions someone else.

observing (ub-ZER-ving) Noticing or paying attention to.

organize (OR-guh-nyz) To put things in order or to make rules.

outline (OWT-lyn) A written description that includes the main points of a paper.

plagiarism (PLAY-juh-ryz-um) Passing off someone else's work as your own.

search engine (SERCH EN-jin) A computer program that searches the Internet for websites.

sources (SORS-ez) Things that give facts or knowledge.

topic (TAH-pik) The subject of a piece of writing.

INDEX

A
answers, 6

B
bibliography, 19
book(s), 8–10, 14, 19

C
categories, 16

E
encyclopedias, 8

G
grizzly bears, 4
group(s), 4, 13, 16, 20

I
interview(s), 6, 14

L
life, 6

O
outline, 14

P
parents, 6
plagiarism, 18–19

Q
question(s), 6,
16–17, 20

R
report(s), 4, 16,
18–19, 22

S
search engine, 10
source(s), 8–9, 12,
19, 22

T
teacher(s), 4, 20
topic(s), 4–6, 8, 10, 22

W
website(s), 10,
12–14, 22

WEBSITES

Due to the changing nature of Internet links, PowerKids Press has developed an online list of websites related to the subject of this book. This site is updated regularly. Please use this link to access the list: www.powerkidslinks.com/cws/inform/